THE SCHOOL AND SOCIETY

THE SCHOOL AND SOCIETY

BEING THREE LECTURES

BY

JOHN DEWEY

***SUPPLEMENTED* BY A STATEMENT OF THE UNIVERSITY ELEMENTARY SCHOOL**

KALPAZ

ISBN: 978-93-5128-872-5(PB)

First Published in 1899
Indian Reprint in 2017

Published by

Kalpaz Publications
C-30, Satyawati Nagar,
Delhi – 110052
E-mail: kalpaz@hotmail.com
Website: kalpazpublications.com
Ph.: +91-9212142040

CONTENTS

LIST OF ILLUSTRATIONS

PUBLISHER'S NOTE

THE three lectures presented in the following pages were delivered before an audience of parents and others interested in the University Elementary School, in the month of April of the year 1899. Mr. Dewey revised them in part from a stenographic report, and unimportant changes and the slight adaptations necessary for the press have been made in his absence. The lectures retain therefore the unstudied character as well as the power of the spoken word. As they imply more or less familiarity with the work of the Elementary School, Mr. Dewey's supplementary statement of this has been added.

AUTHOR'S NOTE

A SECOND edition affords a grateful opportunity for recalling that this little book is a sign of the coöperating thoughts and sympathies of many persons. Its indebtedness to Mrs. Emmons Blaine is partly indicated in the dedication. From my friends, Mr. and Mrs. George Herbert Mead, came that interest, unflagging attention to detail, and artistic taste which, in my absence, remade colloquial remarks until they were fit to print, and then saw the results through the press with the present attractive result — a mode of authorship made easy, which I recommend to others fortunate enough to possess such friends.

It would be an extended paragraph which should list all the friends whose timely and persisting generosity has made possible the school which inspired and defined the ideas of these pages. These friends, I am sure, would be the first to recognize the peculiar appropriateness of especial mention of the names of Mrs. Charles R. Crane and Mrs. William R. Linn.

And the school itself in its educational work is a joint undertaking. Many have engaged in shaping it. The clear and experienced intelligence of my wife is wrought everywhere into its texture. The wisdom, tact and devotion of its instructors have brought about a transformation of its original amorphous plans into articulate form and substance with life and movement of their own. Whatever the issue of the ideas presented in this book, the satisfaction coming from the coöperation of the diverse thoughts and deeds of many persons in undertaking to enlarge the life of the child will abide.

January 5, 1900

THE SCHOOL AND SOCIAL PROGRESS

I

THE SCHOOL AND SOCIAL PROGRESS

We are apt to look at the school from an individualistic standpoint, as something between teacher and pupil, or between teacher and parent. That which interests us most is naturally the progress made by the individual child of our acquaintance, his normal physical development, his advance in ability to read, write, and figure, his growth in the knowledge of geography and history, improvement in manners, habits of promptness, order, and industry — it is from such standards as these that we judge the work of the school. And rightly so. Yet the range of the outlook needs to be enlarged. What the best and wisest parent wants for his own child, that must the community want for all of its children. Any other ideal for our schools is narrow and unlovely; acted upon, it destroys our democracy. All that society has accomplished for itself is put, through the agency of the school, at the disposal of its future members. All its better thoughts of itself it hopes to realize through the new possibilities thus opened to its future self. Here individualism and socialism are at one. Only by being true to the full growth of all the individuals who make it up, can society by any chance be true to itself. And in the self-direction thus given, nothing counts as much as the school, for, as Horace Mann said, "Where anything is growing, one former is worth a thousand re-formers."

Whenever we have in mind the discussion of a new movement in education, it is especially necessary to take the broader, or social view. Otherwise, changes in the school institution and tradition will be looked at as the arbitrary inventions of particular teachers; at the worst transitory fads, and at the best merely improvements in certain details—and this is the plane upon which it is too customary to consider school changes. It is as rational to conceive of the locomotive or the telegraph as personal devices. The modification going on in the method and curriculum of education is as much a product of the changed social situation, and as much an effort to meet the needs of the new society that is forming, as are changes in modes of industry and commerce.

It is to this, then, that I especially ask your attention: the effort to conceive what roughly may be termed the "New Education" in the light of larger changes in society. Can we connect this "New Education" with the general march of events? If we can, it will lose its isolated character, and will cease to be an affair which proceeds only from the over-ingenious minds of pedagogues dealing with particular pupils. It will appear as part and parcel of the whole social evolution, and, in its more general features at least, as inevitable. Let us then ask after the main aspects of the social movement; and afterwards turn to the school to find what witness it gives of effort to put itself in line. And since it is quite impossible to cover the whole ground, I shall for the most part confine myself to one typical thing in the modern school movement—that which passes under the name of manual training, hoping if the relation of that to changed social conditions appears, we shall be ready to concede the point as well regarding other educational innovations.

I make no apology for not dwelling at length upon the social changes in question. Those I shall mention are writ so large that he who runs may read. The change that comes first to mind, the one that overshadows and even controls all others, is the industrial one—the application of science resulting in the great inventions that have utilized the forces of nature on a vast and inexpensive scale: the growth of a world-wide market as the object of production, of vast manufacturing centers to supply this market, of cheap and rapid means of communication and distribution between all its parts. Even as to its feebler beginnings, this change is not much more than a century old; in many of its most important aspects it falls within the short span of those now living. One can hardly believe there has been a revolution in all history so rapid, so extensive, so complete. Through it the face of the earth is making over, even as to its physical forms; political boundaries are wiped out and moved about, as if they were indeed only lines on a paper map; population is hurriedly gathered into cities from the ends of the earth; habits of living are altered with startling abruptness and thoroughness; the search for the truths of nature is infinitely stimulated and facilitated and their application to life made not only practicable, but commercially necessary. Even our moral and religious ideas and interests, the most conservative because the deepest-lying things in our nature, are profoundly affected. That this revolution should not affect education in other than formal and superficial fashion is inconceivable.

Back of the factory system lies the household and neighborhood system. Those of us who are here today need go back only one, two, or at most three generations, to find a time when the household was practically the center in which were carried on, or about which were clustered, all the typical forms of industrial occupation.

The clothing worn was for the most part not only made in the house, but the members of the household were usually familiar with the shearing of the sheep, the carding and spinning of the wool, and the plying of the loom. Instead of pressing a button and flooding the house with electric light, the whole process of getting illumination was followed in its toilsome length, from the killing of the animal and the trying of fat, to the making of wicks and dipping of candles. The supply of flour, of lumber, of foods, of building materials, of household furniture, even of metal ware, of nails, hinges, hammers, etc., was in the immediate neighborhood, in shops which were constantly open to inspection and often centers of neighborhood congregation. The entire industrial process stood revealed, from the production on the farm of the raw materials, till the finished article was actually put to use. Not only this, but practically every member of the household had his own share in the work. The children, as they gained in strength and capacity, were gradually initiated into the mysteries of the several processes. It was a matter of immediate and personal concern, even to the point of actual participation.

We cannot overlook the factors of discipline and of character-building involved in this: training in habits of order and of industry, and in the idea of responsibility, of obligation to do something, to produce something, in the world. There was always something which really needed to be done, and a real necessity that each member of the household should do his own part faithfully and in coöperation with others. Personalities which became effective in action were bred and tested in the medium of action. Again, we cannot overlook the importance for educational purposes of the close and intimate acquaintance got with nature at first hand, with real things and materials, with the actual processes of their manipulation, and the knowledge of their social necessities and uses. In all this there was continual training of observation, of ingenuity, constructive imagination, of logical thought, and of the sense of reality acquired through first-hand contact with actualities. The educative forces of the domestic spinning and weaving, of the saw-mill, the grist-mill, the cooper shop, and the blacksmith forge, were continuously operative.

No number of object-lessons, got up *as* object-lessons for the sake of giving information, can afford even the shadow of a substitute for acquaintance with the plants and animals of the farm and garden, acquired through actual living among them and caring for them. No training of sense-organs in school, introduced for the sake of training, can begin to compete with the alertness and fullness of sense-life that comes through daily intimacy and interest in familiar occupations. Verbal memory can be trained in committing tasks, a certain discipline of the reasoning powers can be acquired through lessons in science and mathematics; but, after all, this is somewhat remote and shadowy compared with the training of attention and of judgment that is acquired in having to do things with a real motive behind and a real outcome ahead. At present, concentration of industry and division of labor have practically eliminated household and neighborhood occupations—at least for educational purposes. But it is useless to bemoan the departure of the good old days of children's modesty, reverence, and implicit obedience, if we expect merely by bemoaning and by exhortation to bring them back. It is radical conditions which have changed, and only an equally radical change in education suffices. We must recognize our compensations — the increase in toleration, in breadth of social judgment, the larger acquaintance with human nature, the sharpened alertness in reading signs of character and interpreting social situations, greater accuracy of adaptation to differing personalities, contact with greater commercial activities. These considerations mean much to the city-bred child of today. Yet there is a real problem: how shall we retain these advantages, and yet introduce into the school something representing the other side of life—occupations which exact personal responsibilities and which train the child with relation to the physical realities of life?

When we turn to the school, we find that one of the most striking tendencies at present is toward the introduction of so-called manual training, shop-work, and the household arts—sewing and cooking.

This has not been done "on purpose," with a full consciousness that the school must now supply that factor of training formerly taken care of in the home, but rather by instinct, by experimenting and finding that such work takes a vital hold of pupils and gives them something which was not to be got in any other way. Consciousness of its real import is still so weak that the work is often done in a half-hearted, confused, and unrelated way. The reasons assigned to justify it are painfully inadequate or sometimes even positively wrong.

If we were to cross-examine even those who are most favorably disposed to the introduction of this work into our school system, we should, I imagine, generally find the main reasons to be that such work engages the full spontaneous interest and attention of the children. It keeps them alert and active, instead of passive and receptive; it makes them more useful, more capable, and hence more inclined to be helpful at home; it prepares them to some extent for the practical duties of later life — the girls to be more efficient house managers, if not actually cooks and sempstresses; the boys (were our educational system only adequately rounded out into trade schools) for their future vocations. I do not underestimate the worth of these reasons. Of those indicated by the changed attitude of the children I shall indeed have something to say in my next talk, when speaking directly of the relationship of the school to the child. But the point of view is, upon the whole, unnecessarily narrow. We must conceive of work in wood and metal, of weaving, sewing, and cooking, as methods of life not as distinct studies.

We must conceive of them in their social significance, as types of the processes by which society keeps itself going, as agencies for bringing home to the child some of the primal necessities of community life, and as ways in which these needs have been met by the growing insight and ingenuity of man; in short, as instrumentalities through which the school itself shall be made a genuine form of active community life, instead of a place set apart in which to learn lessons.

A society is a number of people held together because they are working along common lines, in a common spirit, and with reference to common aims. The common needs and aims demand a growing interchange of thought and growing unity of sympathetic feeling. The radical reason that the present school cannot organize itself as a natural social unit is because just this element of common and productive activity is absent. Upon the playground, in game and sport, social organization takes place spontaneously and inevitably. There is something to do, some activity to be carried on, requiring natural divisions of labor, selection of leaders and followers, mutual coöperation and emulation. In the schoolroom the motive and the cement of social organization are alike wanting. Upon the ethical side, the tragic weakness of the present school is that it endeavors to prepare future members of the social order in a medium in which the conditions of the social spirit are eminently wanting.

The difference that appears when occupations are made the articulating centers of school life is not easy to describe in words; it is a difference in motive, of spirit and atmosphere. As one enters a busy kitchen in which a group of children are actively engaged in the preparation of food, the psychological difference, the change from more or less passive and inert recipiency and restraint to one of buoyant outgoing energy, is so obvious as fairly to strike one in the face. Indeed, to those whose image of the school is rigidly set the change is sure to give a shock. But the change in the social attitude is equally marked. The mere absorption of facts and truths is so exclusively individual an affair that it tends very naturally to pass into selfishness. There is no obvious social motive for the acquirement of mere learning, there is no clear social gain in success thereat. Indeed, almost the only measure for success is a competitive one, in the bad sense of that term—a comparison of results in the recitation or in the examination to see which child has succeeded in getting ahead of others in storing up, in accumulating the maximum of information. So thoroughly is this the prevalent atmosphere that for one child to help another in his task has become a school crime. Where the school work consists in simply learning lessons, mutual assistance, instead of being the most natural form of coöperation and association, becomes a clandestine effort to relieve one's neighbor of his proper duties. Where active work is going on all this is changed. Helping others, instead of being a form of charity which impoverishes the recipient, is simply an aid in setting free the powers and furthering the impulse of the one helped. A spirit of free communication, of interchange of ideas, suggestions, results, both successes and failures of previous experiences, becomes the dominating note of the recitation. So far as emulation enters in, it is in the comparison of individuals, not with regard to the quantity of information personally absorbed, but with reference to the quality of work done—the genuine community standard of value. In an informal but all the more pervasive way, the school life organizes itself on a social basis.

Within this organization is found the principle of school discipline or order. Of course, order is simply a thing which is relative to an end. If you have the end in view of forty or fifty children learning certain set lessons, to be recited to a teacher, your discipline must be devoted to securing that result. But if the end in view is the development of a spirit of social coöperation and community life, discipline must grow out of and be relative to this. There is little order of one sort where things are in process of construction; there is a certain disorder in any busy workshop; there is not silence; persons are not engaged in maintaining certain fixed physical postures; their arms are not folded; they are not holding their books thus and so. They are doing a variety of things, and there is the confusion, the bustle, that results from activity. But out of occupation, out of doing things that are to produce results, and out of doing these in a social and coöperative way, there is born a discipline of its own kind and type. Our whole conception of school discipline changes when we get this point of view. In critical moments we all realize that the only discipline that stands by us, the only training that becomes intuition, is that got through life itself. That we learn from experience, and from books or the sayings of others *only* as they are related to experience, are not mere phrases. But the school has been so set apart, so isolated from the ordinary conditions and motives of life, that the place where children are sent for discipline is the one place in the world where it is most difficult to get experience—the mother of all discipline worth the name. It is only where a narrow and fixed image of traditional school discipline dominates, that one is in any danger of overlooking that deeper and infinitely wider discipline that comes from having a part to do in constructive work, in contributing to a result which, social in spirit, is none the less obvious and tangible in form—and hence in a form with reference to which responsibility may be exacted and accurate judgment passed.

The great thing to keep in mind, then, regarding the introduction into the school of various forms of active occupation, is that through them the entire spirit of the school is renewed. It has a chance to affiliate itself with life, to become the child's habitat, where he learns through directed living; instead of being only a place to learn lessons having an abstract and remote reference to some possible living to be done in the future. It gets a chance to be a miniature community, an embryonic society. This is the fundamental fact, and from this arise continuous and orderly sources of instruction. Under the industrial *régime* described, the child, after all, shared in the work, not for the sake of the sharing, but for the sake of the product. The educational results secured were real, yet incidental and dependent. But in the school the typical occupations followed are freed from all economic stress. The aim is not the economic value of the products, but the development of social power and insight. It is this liberation from narrow utilities, this openness to the possibilities of the human spirit that makes these practical activities in the school allies of art and centers of science and history.

The unity of all the sciences is found in geography. The significance of geography is that it presents the earth as the enduring home of the occupations of man. The world without its relationship to human activity is less than a world. Human industry and achievement, apart from their roots in the earth, are not even a sentiment, hardly a name. The earth is the final source of all man's food. It is his continual shelter and protection, the raw material of all his activities, and the home to whose humanizing and idealizing all his achievement returns. It is the great field, the great mine, the great source of the energies of heat, light, and electricity; the great scene of ocean, stream, mountain, and plain, of which all our agriculture and mining and lumbering, all our manufacturing and distributing agencies, are but the partial elements and factors. It is through occupations determined by this environment that mankind has made its historical and political progress. It is through these occupations that the intellectual and emotional interpretation of nature has been developed. It is through what we do in and with the world that we read its meaning and measure its value.

In educational terms, this means that these occupations in the school shall not be mere practical devices or modes of routine employment, the gaining of better technical skill as cooks, sempstresses, or carpenters, but active centers of scientific insight into natural materials and processes, points of departure whence children shall be led out into a realization of the historic development of man. The actual significance of this can be told better through one illustration taken from actual school work than by general discourse.

There is nothing which strikes more oddly upon

the average intelligent visitor than to see boys as well as girls of ten, twelve, and thirteen years of age engaged in sewing and weaving. If we look at this from the standpoint of preparation of the boys for sewing on buttons and making patches, we get a narrow and utilitarian conception — a basis that hardly justifies giving prominence to this sort of work in the school. But if we look at it from another side, we find that this work gives the point of departure from which the child can trace and follow the progress of mankind in history, getting an insight also into the materials used and the mechanical principles involved. In connection with these occupations, the historic development of man is recapitulated. For example, the children are first given the raw material — the flax, the cotton plant, the wool as it comes from the back of the sheep (if we could take them to the place where the sheep are sheared, so much the better). Then a study is made of these materials from the standpoint of their adaptation to the uses to which they may be put. For instance, a comparison of the cotton fiber with wool fiber is made. I did not know until the children told me, that the reason for the late development of the cotton industry as compared with the woolen is, that the cotton fiber is so very difficult to free by hand from the seeds. The children in one group worked thirty minutes freeing cotton fibers from the boll and seeds, and succeeded in getting out less than one ounce. They could easily believe that one person could only gin one pound a day by hand, and could understand why their ancestors wore woolen instead of cotton clothing. Among other things discovered as affecting their relative utilities, was the shortness of the cotton fiber as compared with that of wool, the former being one-tenth of an inch in length, while that of the latter is an inch in length; also that the fibers of cotton are smooth and do not cling together, while the wool has a certain roughness which makes the fibers stick, thus assisting the spinning. The children worked this out for themselves with the actual material, aided by questions and suggestions from the teacher.

They then followed the processes necessary for working the fibers up into cloth. They re-invented the first frame for carding the wool—a couple of boards with sharp pins in them for scratching it out. They re-devised the simplest process for spinning the wool—a pierced stone or some other weight through which the wool is passed, and which as it is twirled draws out the fiber; next the top, which was spun on the floor, while the children kept the wool in their hands until it was gradually drawn out and wound upon it. Then the children are introduced to the invention next in historic order, working it out experimentally, thus seeing its necessity, and tracing its effects, not only upon that particular industry, but upon modes of social life—in this way passing in review the entire process up to the present complete loom, and all that goes with the application of science in the use of our present available powers. I need not speak of the science involved in this—the study of the fibers, of geographical features, the conditions under which raw materials are grown, the great centers of manufacture and distribution, the physics involved in the machinery of production; nor, again, of the historical side—the influence which these inventions have had upon humanity. You can concentrate the history of all mankind into the evolution of the flax, cotton, and wool fibers into clothing. I do not mean that this is the only, or the best, center. But it is true that certain very real and important avenues to the consideration of the history of the race are thus opened—that the mind is introduced to much more fundamental and controlling influences than usually appear in the political and chronological records that pass for history.

Now, what is true of this one instance of fibers used in fabrics (and, of course, I have only spoken of one or two elementary phases of that) is true in its measure of every material used in every occupation, and of the processes employed.

The occupation supplies the child with a genuine motive; it gives him experience at first hand; it brings him into contact with realities. It does all this, but in addition it is liberalized throughout by translation into its historic values and scientific equivalencies. With the growth of the child's mind in power and knowledge it ceases to be a pleasant occupation merely, and becomes more and more a medium, an instrument, an organ—and is thereby transformed.

This, in turn, has its bearing upon the teaching of science. Under present conditions, all activity, to be successful, has to be directed somewhere and somehow by the scientific expert—it is a case of applied science. This connection should determine its place in education. It is not only that the occupations, the so-called manual or industrial work in the school, give the opportunity for the introduction of science which illuminates them, which makes them material, freighted with meaning, instead of being mere devices of hand and eye; but that the scientific insight thus gained becomes an indispensable instrument of free and active participation in modern social life. Plato somewhere speaks of the slave as one who in his actions does not express his own ideas, but those of some other man. It is our social problem now, even more urgent than in the time of Plato, that method, purpose, understanding, shall exist in the consciousness of the one who does the work, that his activity shall have meaning to himself.

When occupations in the school are conceived in this broad and generous way, I can only stand lost in wonder at the objections so often heard, that such occupations are out of place in the school because they are materialistic, utilitarian, or even menial in their tendency. It sometimes seems to me that those who make these objections must live in quite another world. The world in which most of us live is a world in which everyone has a calling and occupation, something to do. Some are managers and others are subordinates. But the great thing for one as for the other is that each shall have had the education which enables him to see within his daily work all there is in it of large and human significance. How many of the employed are today mere appendages to the machines which they operate! This may be due in part to the machine itself, or to the *régime* which lays so much stress upon the products of the machine; but it is certainly due in large part to the fact that the worker has had no opportunity to develop his imagination and his sympathetic insight as to the social and scientific values found in his work. At present, the impulses which lie at the basis of the industrial system are either practically neglected or positively distorted during the school period. Until the instincts of construction and production are systematically laid hold of in the years of childhood and youth, until they are trained in social directions, enriched by historical interpretation, controlled and illuminated by scientific methods, we certainly are in no position even to locate the source of our economic evils, much less to deal with them effectively.

If we go back a few centuries, we find a practical monopoly of learning. The term *possession* of learning was, indeed, a happy one. Learning was a class matter. This was a necessary result of social conditions. There were not in existence any means by which the multitude could possibly have access to intellectual resources. These were stored up and hidden away in manuscripts. Of these there were at best only a few, and it required long and toilsome preparation to be able to do anything with them. A high-priesthood of learning, which guarded the treasury of truth and which doled it out to the masses under severe restrictions, was the inevitable expression of these conditions. But, as a direct result of the industrial revolution of which we have been speaking, this has been changed. Printing was invented; it was made commercial. Books, magazines, papers were multiplied and cheapened. As a result of the locomotive and telegraph, frequent, rapid, and cheap intercommunication by mails and electricity was called into being. Travel has been rendered easy; freedom of movement, with its accompanying exchange of ideas, indefinitely facilitated. The result has been an intellectual revolution. Learning has been put into circulation. While there still is, and probably always will be, a particular class having the special business of inquiry in hand, a distinctively learned class is henceforth out of the question. It is an anachronism. Knowledge is no longer an immobile solid; it has been liquefied. It is actively moving in all the currents of society itself.

It is easy to see that this revolution, as regards the materials of knowledge, carries with it a marked change in the attitude of the individual. Stimuli of an intellectual sort pour in upon us in all kinds of ways. The merely intellectual life, the life of scholarship and of learning, thus gets a very altered value. Academic and scholastic, instead of being titles of honor, are becoming terms of reproach.

But all this means a necessary change in the attitude of the school, one of which we are as yet far from realizing the full force. Our school methods, and to a very considerable extent our curriculum, are inherited from the period when learning and command of certain symbols, affording as they did the only access to learning, were all-important. The ideals of this period are still largely in control, even where the outward methods and studies have been changed. We sometimes hear the introduction of manual training, art and science into the elementary, and even the secondary schools, deprecated on the ground that they tend toward the production of specialists—that they detract from our present scheme of generous, liberal culture. The point of this objection would be ludicrous if it were not often so effective as to make it tragic. It is our present education which is highly specialized, one-sided and narrow. It is an education dominated almost entirely by the mediæval conception of learning. It is something which appeals for the most part simply to the intellectual aspect of our natures, our desire to learn, to accumulate information, and to get control of the symbols of learning; not to our impulses and tendencies to make, to do, to create, to produce, whether in the form of utility or of art. The very fact that manual training, art and science are objected to as technical, as tending toward mere specialism, is of itself as good testimony as could be offered to the specialized aim which controls current education. Unless education had been virtually identified with the exclusively intellectual pursuits, with learning as such, all these materials and methods would be welcome, would be greeted with the utmost hospitality.

While training for the profession of learning is regarded as the type of culture, as a liberal education, that of a mechanic, a musician, a lawyer, a doctor, a farmer, a merchant, or a railroad manager is regarded as purely technical and professional. The result is that which we see about us everywhere — the division into "cultured" people and "workers," the separation of theory and practice. Hardly one per cent. of the entire school population ever attains to what we call higher education; only five per cent. to the grade of our high school; while much more than half leave on or before the completion of the fifth year of the elementary grade. The simple facts of the case are that in the great majority of human beings the distinctively intellectual interest is not dominant. They have the so-called practical impulse and disposition. In many of those in whom by nature intellectual interest is strong, social conditions prevent its adequate realization. Consequently by far the larger number of pupils leave school as soon as they have acquired the rudiments of learning, as soon as they have enough of the symbols of reading, writing, and calculating to be of practical use to them in getting a living. While our educational leaders are talking of culture, the development of personality, etc., as the end and aim of education, the great majority of those who pass under the tuition of the school regard it only as a narrowly practical tool with which to get bread and butter enough to eke out a restricted life. If we were to conceive our educational end and aim in a less exclusive way, if we were to introduce into educational processes the activities which appeal to those whose dominant interest is to do and to make, we should find the hold of the school upon its members to be more vital, more prolonged, containing more of culture.

But why should I make this labored presentation? The obvious fact is that our social life has undergone a thorough and radical change. If our education is to have any meaning for life, it must pass through an equally complete transformation. This transformation is not something to appear suddenly, to be executed in a day by conscious purpose. It is already in progress. Those modifications of our school system which often appear (even to those most actively concerned with them, to say nothing of their spectators) to be mere changes of detail, mere improvement within the school mechanism, are in reality signs and evidences of evolution. The introduction of active occupations, of nature study, of elementary science, of art, of history; the relegation of the merely symbolic and formal to a secondary position; the change in the moral school atmosphere, in the relation of pupils and teachers—of discipline; the introduction of more active, expressive, and self-directing factors — all these are not mere accidents, they are necessities of the larger social evolution. It remains but to organize all these factors, to appreciate them in their fullness of meaning, and to put the ideas and ideals involved into complete, uncompromising possession of our school system. To do this means to make each one of our schools an embryonic community life, active with types of occupations that reflect the life of the larger society, and permeated throughout with the spirit of art, history, and science. When the school introduces and trains each child of society into membership within such a little community, saturating him with the spirit of service, and providing him with the instruments of effective self-direction, we shall have the deepest and best guarantee of a larger society which is worthy, lovely, and harmonious.

THE SCHOOL AND THE LIFE OF THE CHILD

II

THE SCHOOL AND THE LIFE OF THE CHILD

Last week I tried to put before you the relationship between the school and the larger life of the community, and the necessity for certain changes in the methods and materials of school work, that it might be better adapted to present social needs.

Today I wish to look at the matter from the other side, and consider the relationship of the school to the life and development of the children in the school. As it is difficult to connect general principles with such thoroughly concrete things as little children, I have taken the liberty of introducing a good deal of illustrative matter from the work of the University Elementary School, that in some measure you may appreciate the way in which the ideas presented work themselves out in actual practice.

Some few years ago I was looking about the school supply stores in the city, trying to find desks and chairs which seemed thoroughly suitable from all points of view—artistic, hygienic, and educational—to the needs of the children. We had a good deal of difficulty in finding what we needed, and finally one dealer, more intelligent than the rest, made this remark: "I am afraid we have not what you want. You want something at which the children may work; these are all for listening." That tells the story of the traditional education. Just as the biologist can take a bone or two and reconstruct the whole animal, so, if we put before the mind's eye the ordinary schoolroom, with its rows of ugly desks placed in geometrical order, crowded together so that there shall be as little moving room as possible, desks almost all of the same size, with just space enough to hold books, pencils and paper, and add a table, some chairs, the bare walls, and possibly a few pictures, we can reconstruct the only educational activity that can possibly go on in such a place. It is all made "for listening"—for simply studying lessons out of a book is only another kind of listening; it marks the dependency of one mind upon another. The attitude of listening means, comparatively speaking, passivity, absorption; that there are certain ready-made materials which are there, which have been prepared by the school superintendent, the board, the teacher, and of which the child is to take in as much as possible in the least possible time.

There is very little place in the traditional schoolroom for the child to work. The workshop, the laboratory, the materials, the tools with which the child may construct, create, and actively inquire, and even the requisite space, have been for the most part lacking. The things that have to do with these processes have not even a definitely recognized place in education. They are what the educational authorities who write editorials in the daily papers generally term "fads" and "frills." A lady told me yesterday that she had been visiting different schools trying to find one where activity on the part of the children preceded the giving of information on the part of the teacher, or where the children had some motive for demanding the information. She visited, she said, twenty-four different schools before she found her first instance. I may add that that was not in this city.

Another thing that is suggested by these schoolrooms, with their set desks, is that everything is arranged for handling as large numbers of children as possible; for dealing with children *en masse*, as an aggregate of units; involving, again, that they be treated passively. The moment children act they individualize themselves; they cease to be a mass, and become the intensely distinctive beings that we are acquainted with out of school. in the home, the family, on the playground, and in the neighborhood.

On the same basis is explicable the uniformity of method and curriculum. If everything is on a "listening" basis, you can have uniformity of material and method. The ear, and the book which reflects the ear, constitute the medium which is alike for all. There is next to no opportunity for adjustment to varying capacities and demands. There is a certain amount—a fixed quantity—of ready-made results and accomplishments to be acquired by all children alike in a given time. It is in response to this demand that the curriculum has been developed from the elementary school up through the college. There is just so much desirable knowledge, and there are just so many needed technical accomplishments in the world. Then comes the mathematical problem of dividing this by the six, twelve, or sixteen years of school life. Now give the children every year just the proportionate fraction of the total, and by the time they have finished they will have mastered the whole. By covering so much ground during this hour or day or week or year, everything comes out with perfect evenness at the end—provided the children have not forgotten what they have previously learned. The outcome of all this is Matthew Arnold's report of the statement, proudly made to him by an educational authority in France, that so many thousands of children were studying at a given hour, say eleven o'clock, just such a lesson in geography; and in one of our own western cities this proud boast used to be repeated to successive visitors by its superintendent.

I may have exaggerated somewhat in order to make plain the typical points of the old education: its passivity of attitude, its mechanical massing of children, its uniformity of curriculum and method. It may be summed up by stating that the center of gravity is outside the child. It is in the teacher, the text-book, anywhere and everywhere you please except in the immediate instincts and activities of the child himself. On that basis there is not much to be said about the *life* of the child. A good deal might be said about the studying of the child, but the school is not the place where the child *lives*. Now the change which is coming into our education is the shifting of the center of gravity. It is a change, a revolution, not unlike that introduced by Copernicus when the astronomical center shifted from the earth to the sun. In this case the child becomes the sun about which the appliances of education revolve; he is the center about which they are organized.

If we take an example from an ideal home, where the parent is intelligent enough to recognize what is best for the child, and is able to supply what is needed, we find the child learning through the social converse and constitution of the family. There are certain points of interest and value to him in the conversation carried on:

statements are made, inquiries arise, topics are discussed, and the child continually learns. He states his experiences, his misconceptions are corrected. Again the child participates in the household occupations, and thereby gets habits of industry, order, and regard for the rights and ideas of others, and the fundamental habit of subordinating his activities to the general interest of the household. Participation in these household tasks becomes an opportunity for gaining knowledge. The ideal home would naturally have a workshop where the child could work out his constructive instincts. It would have a miniature laboratory in which his inquiries could be directed. The life of the child would extend out of doors to the garden, surrounding fields, and forests. He would have his excursions, his walks and talks, in which the larger world out of doors would open to him.

Now, if we organize and generalize all of this, we have the ideal school. There is no mystery about it, no wonderful discovery of pedagogy or educational theory. It is simply a question of doing systematically and in a large, intelligent, and competent way what for various reasons can be done in most households only in a comparatively meager and haphazard manner. In the first place, the ideal home has to be enlarged. The child must be brought into contact with more grown people and with more children in order that there may be the freest and richest social life. Moreover, the occupations and relationships of the home environment are not specially selected for the growth of the child; the main object is something else, and what the child can get out of them is incidental. Hence the need of a school. In this school the life of the child becomes the all-controlling aim. All the media necessary to further the growth of the child center there. Learning?—certainly, but living primarily, and learning through and in relation to this living. When we take the life of the child centered and organized in this way, we do not find that he is first of all a listening being; quite the contrary.

The statement so frequently made that education means "drawing out" is excellent, if we mean simply to contrast it with the process of pouring in. But, after all, it is difficult to connect the idea of drawing out with the ordinary doings of the child of three, four, seven, or eight years of age. He is already running over, spilling over, with activities of all kinds. He is not a purely latent being whom the adult has to approach with great caution and skill in order gradually to draw out some hidden germ of activity. The child is already intensely active, and the question of education is the question of taking hold of his activities, of giving them direction. Through direction, through organized use, they tend toward valuable results, instead of scattering or being left to merely impulsive expression.

If we keep this before us, the difficulty I find uppermost in the minds of many people regarding what is termed the new education is not so much solved as dissolved; it disappears. A question often asked is: if you begin with the child's ideas, impulses and interests, all so crude, so random and scattering, so little refined or spiritualized, how is he going to get the necessary discipline, culture and information? If there were no way open to us except to excite and indulge these impulses of the child, the question might well be asked. We should either have to ignore and repress the activities, or else to humor them. But if we have organization of equipment and of materials, there is another path open to us. We can direct the child's activities, giving them exercise along certain lines, and can thus lead up to the goal which logically stands at the end of the paths followed.

"If wishes were horses, beggars would ride." Since they are not, since really to satisfy an impulse or interest means to work it out, and working it out involves running up against obstacles, becoming acquainted with materials, exercising ingenuity, patience, persistence, alertness, it of necessity involves discipline—ordering of power

—and supplies knowledge. Take the example of the little child who wants to make a box. If he stops short with the imagination or wish, he certainly will not get discipline. But when he attempts to realize his impulse, it is a question of making his idea definite, making it into a plan, of taking the right kind of wood, measuring the parts needed, giving them the necessary proportions, etc. There is involved the preparation of materials, the sawing, planing, the sand-papering, making all the edges and corners to fit. Knowledge of tools and processes is inevitable. If the child realizes his instinct and makes the box, there is plenty of opportunity to gain discipline and perseverance, to exercise effort in overcoming obstacles, and to attain as well a great deal of information.

So undoubtedly the little child who thinks he would like to cook has little idea of what it means or costs, or what it requires. It is simply a desire to "mess around," perhaps to imitate the activities of older people. And it is doubtless possible to let ourselves down to that level and simply humor that interest. But here, too, if the impulse is exercised, utilized, it runs up against the actual world of hard conditions, to which it must accommodate itself; and there again come in the factors of discipline and knowledge. One of the children became impatient recently, at having to work things out by a long method of experimentation, and said: "Why do we bother with this? Let's follow a recipe in a cook-book." The teacher asked the children where the recipe came from, and the conversation showed that if they simply followed this they would not understand the reasons for what they were doing. They were then quite willing to go on with the experimental work. To follow that work will, indeed, give an illustration of just the point in question. Their occupation happened that day to be the cooking of eggs, as making a transition from the cooking of vegetables to that of meats. In order to get a basis of comparison they first summarized the constituent food elements in the vegetables and made a preliminary comparison with those found in meat. Thus they found that the woody fiber or cellulose in vegetables corresponded to the connective tissue in meat, giving the element of form and structure. They found that starch and starchy products were characteristic of the vegetables, that mineral salts were found in both alike, and that there was fat in both — a small quantity in vegetable food and a large amount in animal. They were prepared then to take up the study of albumen as the characteristic feature of animal food, corresponding to starch in the vegetables, and were ready to consider the conditions requisite for the proper

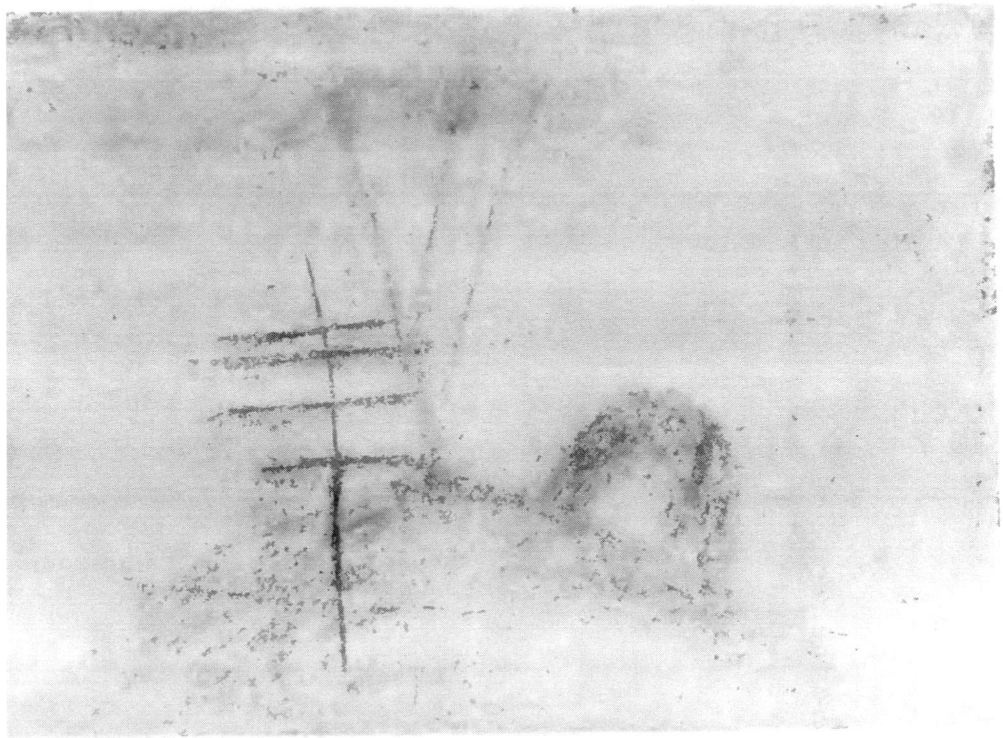

CHILD'S DRAWING OF A CAVE AND TREES

treatment of albumen — the eggs serving as the material of experiment.

They experimented first by taking water at various temperatures, finding out when it was scalding, simmering, and boiling hot, and ascertained the effect of the various degrees of temperature on the white of the egg. That worked out, they were prepared, not simply to cook eggs, but to understand the principle involved in the cooking of eggs. I do not wish to lose sight of the universal in the particular incident. For the child simply to desire to cook an egg, and accordingly drop it in water for three minutes, and take it out when he is told, is not educative. But for the child to realize his own impulse by recognizing the facts, materials and conditions involved, and then to regulate his impulse through that recognition, is educative. This is the difference, upon which I wish to insist, between exciting or indulging an interest and realizing it through its direction.

Another instinct of the child is the use of pencil and paper. All children like to express themselves through the medium of form and color. If you simply indulge this interest by letting the child go on indefinitely, there is no growth that is more than accidental. But let the child first express his impulse, and then through criticism, question, and suggestion bring him to consciousness of what he has done, and what he needs to do, and the result is quite different. Here, for example, is the work of a seven-year-old child. It is not average work, it is the best work done among the little children, but it illustrates the particular principle of which I have been speaking. They had been talking about the primitive conditions of social life when people lived in caves. The child's idea of that found expression in this way: the cave is neatly set up on the hill side in an impossible way. You see the conventional tree of childhood; a vertical line with horizontal branches on each side. If the child had been allowed to go on repeating this sort of thing day by day, he would be indulging his instinct rather than exercising it. But the child was now asked to look closely at trees, to compare those seen with the one drawn, to examine more closely and consciously into the conditions of his work. Then he drew trees from observation.

Finally he drew again from combined observation, memory, and imagination. He made again a free illustration, expressing his own imaginative thought, but controlled by detailed study of actual trees. The result was a scene representing a bit of forest; so far as it goes, it seems to me to have as much poetic feeling as the work of an adult, while at the same time its trees are, in

CHILD'S DRAWING OF A FOREST

their proportions possible ones, not mere symbols.

If we roughly classify the impulses which are available in the school, we may group them under four heads. There is the social instinct of the children as shown in conversation, personal intercourse, and communication. We all know how self-centered the little child is at the age of four or five. If any new subject is brought up, if he says anything at all, it is: "I have seen that;" or, "My papa or mamma told me about that." His horizon is not large; an experience must come immediately home to him, if he is to be sufficiently interested to relate it to others and seek theirs in return. And yet the egoistic and limited interest of little children is in this manner capable of infinite expansion. The language instinct is the simplest form of the social expression of the child. Hence it is a great, perhaps the greatest of all educational resources.

Then there is the instinct of making—the constructive impulse. The child's impulse to do finds expression first in play, in movement, gesture, and make-believe, becomes more definite, and seeks outlet in shaping materials into tangible forms and permanent embodiment. The child has not much instinct for abstract inquiry. The instinct of investigation seems to grow out of the combination of the constructive impulse with the conversational. There is no distinction between experimental science for little children and the work done in the carpenter shop. Such work as they can do in physics or chemistry is not for the purpose of making technical generalizations or even arriving at abstract truths. Children simply like to do things, and watch to see what will happen. But this can be taken advantage of, can be directed into ways where it gives results of value, as well as be allowed to go on at random.

And so the expressive impulse of the children, the art instinct, grows also out of the communicating and constructive instincts. It is their refinement and full manifestation. Make the construction adequate, make it full, free, and flexible, give it a social motive, something to tell, and you have a work of art. Take one illustration of this in connection with the textile work—sewing and weaving. The children made a primitive loom in the shop; here the constructive instinct was appealed to. Then they wished to do something with this loom, to make something. It was the type of the Indian loom, and they were shown blankets woven by the Indians. Each child made a design kindred in idea to those of the Navajo blankets, and the one which seemed best adapted to the work in hand was selected. The technical resources were limited, but the coloring and form

CHILD'S DRAWING OF HANDS SPINNING

were worked out by the children. The example shown was made by the twelve-year-old children. Examination shows that it took patience, thoroughness, and perseverance to do the work. It involved not merely discipline and information of both a historical sort and the elements of technical design, but also something of the spirit of art in adequately conveying an idea.

One more instance of the connection of the art side with the constructive side. The children had been studying primitive spinning and carding, when one of them, twelve years of age, made a picture of one of the older children spinning. Here is another piece of work which is not quite average; it is better than the average. It is an illustration of two hands and the drawing out of the wool to get it ready for spinning. This was done by a child eleven years of age. But, upon the whole, with the younger children especially, the art impulse is connected mainly with the social instinct — the desire to tell, to represent.

Now, keeping in mind these fourfold interests — the interest in conversation or communication; in inquiry, or finding out things; in making things, or construction; and in artistic expression — we may say they are the natural resources, the uninvested capital, upon the exercise of which depends the active growth of the child. I wish to give one or two illustrations, the first from the work of children seven years of age. It illustrates in a way the dominant desire of the children to talk, particularly about folks and of things in relation to folks. If you observe little children, you will find they are interested in the world of things mainly in its connection with people, as a background and medium of human concerns. Many anthropologists have told us there are certain identities in the child interests with those of primitive life. There is a sort of natural recurrence of the child mind to the typical activities of primitive peoples; witness the hut which the boy likes to build in the yard, playing hunt, with bows, arrows, spears, and so on. Again the question comes: What are we to do with this interest—are we to ignore it, or just excite and draw it out? Or shall we get hold of it and direct it to something ahead, something better? Some of the work that has been planned for our seven-year-old children has the latter end in view—to utilize this interest so that it shall become a means of seeing the progress of the human race. The children begin by imagining present conditions taken away until they are in contact with nature at first hand. That takes them back to a hunting people, to a people living in caves or trees and getting a precarious subsistence by hunting and fishing. They imagine as far as possible the various natural

CHILD'S DRAWING OF A GIRL SPINNING

physical conditions adapted to that sort of life; say, a hilly, woody slope, near mountains and a river where fish would be abundant. Then they go on in imagination through the hunting to the semi-agricultural stage, and through the nomadic to the settled agricultural stage. The point I wish to make is that there is abundant opportunity thus given for actual study, for inquiry which results in gaining information. So, while the instinct primarily appeals to the social side, the interest of the child in people and their doings is carried on into the larger world of reality. For example, the children had some idea of primitive weapons, of the stone arrowhead, etc. That provided occasion for the testing of materials as regards their friability, their shape, texture, etc., resulting in a lesson in mineralogy, as they examined the different stones to find which was best suited to the purpose. The discussion of the iron age supplied a demand for the construction of a smelting oven made out of clay, and of considerable size. As the children did not get their drafts right at first, the mouth of the furnace not being in proper relation to the vent, as to size and position, instruction in the principles of combustion, the nature of drafts and of fuel, was required. Yet the instruction was not given ready-made; it was first needed, and then arrived at experimentally. Then the children took some material, such as copper, and went through a series of experiments, fusing it, working it into objects; and the same experiments were made with lead and other metals. This work has been also a continuous course in geography, since the children have had to imagine and work out the various physical conditions necessary to the different forms of social life implied. What would be the physical conditions appropriate to pastoral life? to the beginning of agriculture? to fishing? What would be the natural method of exchange between these peoples? Having worked out such points in conversation, they have afterward represented them in maps and sand-molding. Thus they have gained ideas of the various forms of the configuration of the earth, and at the same time have seen them in their relation to human activity, so that they are not simply external facts, but are fused and welded with social conceptions regarding the life and progress of humanity. The result, to my mind, justifies completely the conviction that children, in a year of such work (of five hours a week altogether), get indefinitely more acquaintance with facts of science, geography, and anthropology than they get where information is the professed end and object, where they are simply set to learning facts in fixed lessons. As to discipline, they get more training of attention, more power of interpretation, of drawing inferences, of acute observation and continuous reflection, than if they were put to working out arbitrary problems simply for the sake of discipline.

I should like at this point to refer to the recitaton. We all know what it has been—a placer where the child shows off to the teacher and the other children the amount of information he has succeeded in assimilating from the text-book. From this other standpoint, the recitation becomes preëminently a social meeting place; it is to the school what the spontaneous conversation is at home, excepting that it is more organized, following definite lines. The recitation becomes the social clearing-house, where experiences and ideas are exchanged and subjected to criticism, where misconceptions are corrected, and new lines of thought and inquiry are set up.

This change of the recitation from an examination of knowledge already acquired to the free play of the children's communicative instinct, affects and modifies all the language work of the school. Under the old *régime* it was unquestionably a most serious problem to give the children a full and free use of language. The reason was obvious. The natural motive for language was seldom offered. In the pedagogical text-books language is defined as the medium of expressing thought. It becomes that, more or less, to adults with trained minds, but it hardly needs to be said that language is primarily a social thing, a means by which we give our experiences to others and get theirs again in return. When it is taken from its natural basis, it is no wonder that it becomes a complex and difficult problem to teach language. Think of the absurdity of having to teach language as a thing by itself. If there is anything the child will do before he goes to school, it is to talk of the things that interest him. But when there are no vital interests appealed to in the school, when language is used simply for the repetition of lessons, it is not surprising that one of the chief difficulties of school work has come to be instruction in the mother-tongue. Since the language taught is unnatural, not growing out of the real desire to communicate vital impressions and convictions, the freedom of children in its use gradually disappears, until finally the high-school teacher has to invent all kinds of devices to assist in getting any spontaneous and full use of speech. Moreover, when the language instinct is appealed to in a social way, there is a continual contact with reality. The result is that the child always has something in his mind to talk about, he has something to say; he has a thought to express, and a thought is not a thought unless it is one's own. On the traditional method, the child must say something that he has merely learned. There is all the difference in the world between having something to say and having to say something. The child who has a variety of materials and facts wants to talk about them, and his language becomes more refined and full, because it is controlled and informed by realities. Reading and writing, as well as the oral use of language, may be taught on this basis. It can be done in a *related* way, as the outgrowth of the child's social desire to recount his experiences and get in return the experiences of others, directed always through contact with the facts and forces which determine the truth communicated.

I shall not have time to speak of the work of the older children, where the original crude instincts of construction and communication have been developed into something like scientifically directed inquiry, but I will give an illustration of the use of language following upon this experimental work. The work was on the basis of a simple experiment of the commonest sort, gradually leading the children out into geological and geographical study. The sentences that I am going to read seem to me poetic as well as "scientific." "A long time ago when the earth was new, when it was lava, there was no water on the earth, and there was steam all round the earth up in the air, as there were many gases in the air. One of them was carbon dioxide. The steam became clouds, because the earth began to cool off, and after a while it began to rain, and the water came down and dissolved the carbon dioxide from the air." There is a good deal more science in that than probably would be apparent at the outset. It represents some three months of work on the part of the child. The children kept daily and weekly records, but this is part of the summing up of the quarter's work. I call this language poetic, because the child has a clear image and has a personal feeling for the realities imaged. I extract sentences from two other records to illustrate further the vivid use of language when there is a vivid experience back of it. "When the earth was cold enough to condense, the water, with the help of carbon dioxide, *pulls* the calcium out of the rocks into a large body of water where the little animals could get it." The other reads as follows: "When the earth cooled, calcium was in the rocks. Then the carbon dioxide and water united and formed a solution, and, as it ran, it *tore* out the calcium and carried it on to the sea, where there were little animals who took it out of solution." The use of such words as "pulled" and "tore" in connection with the process of chemical combination evidences a personal realization which compels its own appropriate expression.

If I had not taken so much time in my other illustrations, I should like to show how, beginning with very simple material things, the children were led on to larger fields of investigation, and to the intellectual discipline that is the accompaniment of such research. I will simply mention the experiment in which the work began. It consisted in making precipitated chalk, used for polishing metals. The children, with simple apparatus — a tumbler, lime water, and a glass tube — precipitated the calcium carbonate out of the water; and from this beginning went on to a study of the processes by which rocks of various sorts, igneous, sedimentary, etc., had been formed on the surface of the earth and the places they occupy; then to points in the geography of the United States, Hawaii, and Puerto Rico; to the effects of these various bodies of rock, in their various configurations, upon the human occupations; so that this geological record finally rounded itself out into the life of man at the present time. The children saw and felt the connection between these geologic processes taking place ages and ages ago, and the physical conditions determining the industrial occupations of today.

Of all the possibilities involved in the subject, "The School and the Life of the Child," I have selected but one, because I have found that that one gives people more difficulty, is more of a stumbling-block, than any other. One may be ready to admit that it would be most desirable for the school to be a place in which the child should really live, and get a life-experience in which he should delight and find meaning for its own sake. But then we hear this inquiry: how, upon this basis, shall the child get the needed information; how shall he undergo the required discipline? Yes, it has come to this, that with many, if not most, people the normal processes of life appear to be incompatible with getting information and discipline. So I have tried to indicate, in a highly general and inadequate way (for only the school itself, in its daily operation, could give a detailed and worthy representation), how the problem works itself out — how it is possible to lay hold upon the rudimentary instincts of human nature, and, by supplying a proper medium, so control their expression as not only to facilitate and enrich the growth of the individual child, but also to supply the results, and far more, of technical information and discipline that have been the ideals of education in the past.

But although I have selected this especial way of approach (as a concession to the question almost universally raised), I am not willing to leave the matter in this more or less negative and explanatory condition. Life is the great thing after all; the life of the child at its time and in its measure, no less than the life of the adult. Strange would it be, indeed, if intelligent and serious attention to what the child *now* needs and is capable of in the way of a rich, valuable, and expanded life should somehow conflict with the needs and possibilities of later, adult life. "Let us live with our children," certainly means, first of all, that our children shall live — not that they shall be hampered and stunted by being forced into all kinds of conditions, the most remote consideration of which is relevancy to the present life of the child. If we seek the kingdom of heaven, educationally, all other things shall be added unto us — which, being interpreted, is that if we identify ourselves with the real instincts and needs of childhood, and ask only after its fullest assertion and growth, the discipline and information and culture of adult life shall all come in their due season.

Speaking of culture reminds me that in a way I have been speaking only of the outside of the child's activity — only of the outward expression of his impulses toward saying, making, finding out, and creating. The real child, it hardly need be said, lives in the world of imaginative values, and ideas which find only imperfect outward embodiment. We hear much nowadays about the cultivation of the child's "imagination." Then we undo much of our own talk and work by a belief that the imagination is some special part of the child, that finds its satisfaction in some one particular direction—generally speaking, that of the unreal and make-believe, of the myth and made-up story. Why are we so hard of heart and so slow to believe? The imagination is the medium in which the child lives. To him there is everywhere and in everything that occupies his mind and activity at all, a surplusage of value and significance. The question of the relation of the school to the child's life is at bottom simply this: shall we ignore this native setting and tendency, dealing not with the living child at all, but with the dead image we have erected, or shall we give it play and satisfaction? If we once believe in life and in the life of the child, then will all the occupations and uses spoken of, then will all history and science, become instruments of appeal and materials of culture to his imagination, and through that to the richness and the orderliness of his life. Where we now see only the outward doing and the outward product, there, behind all visible results, is the re-adjustment of mental attitude, the enlarged and sympathetic vision, the sense of growing power, and the willing ability to identify both insight and capacity with the interests of the world and man. Unless culture be a superficial polish, a veneering of mahogany over common wood, it surely is this—the growth of the imagination in flexibility, in scope, and in sympathy, till the life which the individual lives is informed with the life of nature and of society. When nature and society can live in the schoolroom, when the forms and tools of learning are subordinated to the substance of experience, then shall there be an opportunity for this identification, and culture shall be the democratic password.

WASTE IN EDUCATION

III

WASTE IN EDUCATION

The subject announced for today was "Waste in Education." I should like first to state briefly its relation to the two preceding lectures. The first dealt with the school in its social aspects, and the necessary re-adjustments that have to be made to render it effective in present social conditions. The second dealt with the school in relation to the growth of individual children. Now the third deals with the school as itself an institution, both in relation to society and to its own members—the children. It deals with the question of organization, because all waste is the result of the lack of it, the motive lying behind organization being promotion of economy and efficiency. This question is not one of the waste of money or the waste of things. These matters count; but the primary waste is that of human life, the life of the children while they are at school, and afterward because of inadequate and perverted preparation.

So, when we speak of organization, we are not to think simply of the externals; of that which goes by the name "school system"—the school board, the superintendent, and the building, the engaging and promotion of teachers, etc. These things enter in, but the fundamental organization is that of the school itself as a community of individuals, in its relations to other forms of social life. All waste is due to isolation. Organization is nothing but getting things into connection with one another, so that they work easily, flexibly, and fully. Therefore in speaking of this question of waste in education, I desire to call your attention to the isolation of the various parts of the school system, to the lack of unity in the aims of education, to the lack of coherence in its studies and methods.

I have made a chart (I) which, while I speak of the isolations of the school system itself, may perhaps appeal to the eye and save a little time in verbal explanations. A paradoxical friend of mine says there is nothing so obscure as an illustration, and it is quite possible that my attempt to illustrate my point will simply prove the truth of his statement.

The blocks represent the various elements in the school system, and are intended to indicate roughly the length of time given to each division, and also the overlapping, both in time and subjects studied, of the individual parts of the system. With each block is given the historical conditions in which it arose and its ruling ideal.

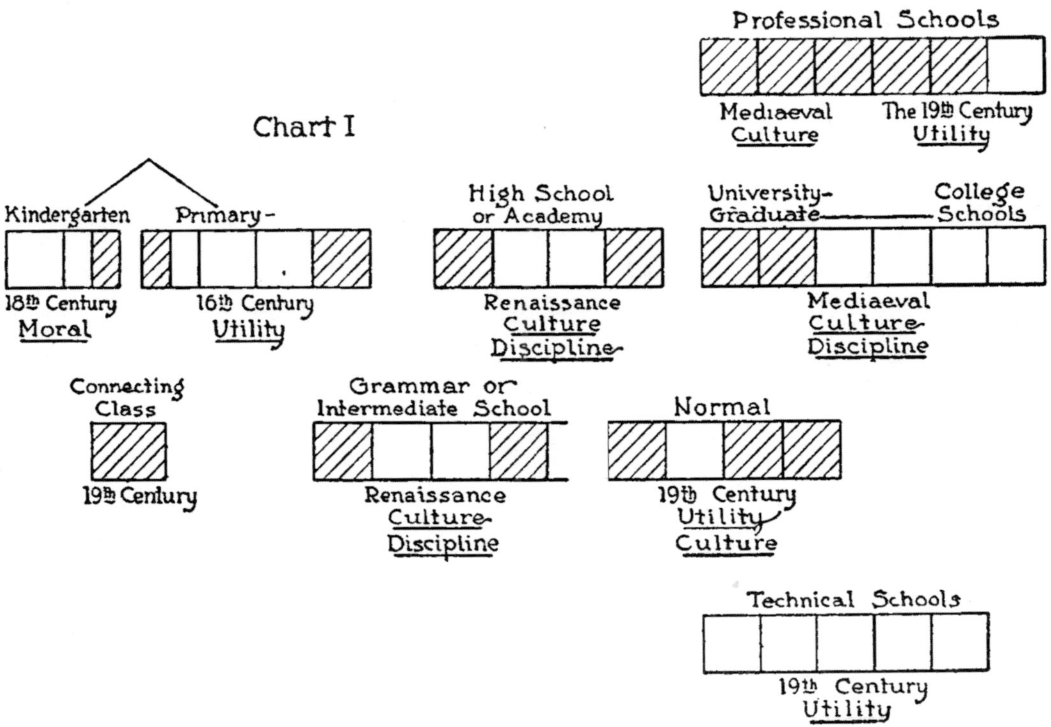
Chart I
Professional Schools
Mediaeval Culture
The 19th Century Utility
Kindergarten
18th Century Moral
Primary-
16th Century Utility
High School or Academy
Renaissance Culture Discipline
University-Graduate
College Schools
Mediaeval Culture Discipline
Connecting Class
19th Century
Grammar or Intermediate School
Renaissance Culture Discipline
Normal
19th Century Utility Culture
Technical Schools
19th Century Utility

The school system, upon the whole, has grown from the top down. During the middle ages it was essentially a cluster of professional schools — especially law and theology. Our present university comes down to us from the middle ages. I will not say that at present it is a mediæval institution, but it had its roots in the middle ages, and it has not outlived all mediæval traditions regarding learning.

The kindergarten, rising with the present century, was a union of the nursery and of the philosophy of Schelling; a wedding of the plays and games which the mother carried on with her children, to Schelling's highly romantic and symbolic philosophy. The elements that came from the actual study of child life — the continuation of the nursery — have remained a life-bringing force in all education; the Schellingesque factors made an obstruction between it and the rest of the school system, brought about isolations.

The line drawn over the top indicates that there is a certain interaction between the kindergarten and the primary school; for, so far as the primary school remained in spirit foreign to the natural interests of child life, it was isolated from the kindergarten, so that it is a problem, at present, to introduce kindergarten methods into the primary school; the problem of the so-called connecting class. The difficulty is that the two are not one from the start. To get a connection the teacher has had to climb over the wall instead of entering in at the gate.

On the side of aims, the ideal of the kindergarten was the moral development of the children, rather than instruction or discipline; an ideal sometimes emphasized to the point of sentimentality. The primary school grew practically out of the popular movement of the sixteenth century, when along with the invention of printing and the growth of commerce, it became a business necessity to know how to read, write, and figure. The aim was distinctly a practical one; it was utility; getting command of these tools, the symbols of learning, not for the sake of learning, but because they gave access to careers in life otherwise closed.

The division next to the primary school is the grammar school. The term is not much used in the West, but is common in the eastern states. It goes back to the time of the revival of learning—a little earlier perhaps than the conditions out of which the primary school originated, and, even when contemporaneous, having a different ideal. It had to do with the study of language in the higher sense; because, at the time of the Renaissance, Latin and Greek connected people with the culture of the past, with the Roman and Greek world. The classic languages were the only means of escape from the limitations of the middle ages. Thus there sprang up the prototype of the grammar school, more liberal than the university (so largely professional in character), for the purpose of putting into the hands of the people the key to the old learning, that men might see a world with a larger horizon. The object was primarily culture, secondarily discipline. It represented much more than the present grammar school. It was the liberal element in the college, which, extending downward, grew into the academy and the high school. Thus the secondary school is still in part just a lower college (having an even higher curriculum than the college of a few centuries ago) or a preparatory department to a college, and in part a rounding up of the utilities of the elementary school.

There appear then two products of the nineteenth century, the technical and normal schools. The schools of technology, engineering, etc., are, of course, mainly the development of nineteenth-century business conditions, as the primary school was the development of business conditions of the sixteenth century. The normal school arose because of the necessity for training teachers, with the idea partly of professional drill, and partly that of culture.

Without going into more detail, we have

some eight different parts of the school system as represented on the chart, all of which arose historically at different times, having different ideals in view, and consequently different methods. I do not wish to suggest that all of the isolation, all of the separation, that has existed in the past between the different parts of the school system still persists. One must, however, recognize that they have never yet been welded into one complete whole. The great problem in education on the administrative side is how to unite these different parts.

Consider the training schools for teachers—the normal schools. These occupy at present a somewhat anomalous position, intermediate between the high school and the college, requiring the high-school preparation, and covering a certain amount of college work. They are isolated from the higher subject-matter of scholarship, since, upon the whole, their object has been to train persons *how* to teach, rather than *what* to teach; while, if we go to the college, we find the other half of this isolation—learning *what* to teach, with almost a contempt for methods of teaching. The college is shut off from contact with children and youth. Its members, to a great extent, away from home and forgetting their own childhood, become eventually teachers with a large amount of subject-matter at command, and little knowledge of how this is related to the minds of those to whom it is to be taught. In this division between what to teach and how to teach, each side suffers from the separation.

It is interesting to follow out the inter-relation between primary, grammar, and high schools. The elementary school has crowded up and taken many subjects previously studied in the old New England grammar school. The high school has pushed its subjects down. Latin and algebra have been put in the upper grades, so that the seventh and eighth grades are, after all, about all that is left of the old grammar school. They are a sort of amorphous composite, being partly a place where children go on learning what they already have learned (to read, write, and figure), and partly a place of preparation for the high school. The name in some parts of New England for these upper grades was "Intermediate School." The term was a happy one; the work was simply intermediate between something that had been and something that was going to be, having no special meaning on its own account.

Just as the parts are separated, so do the ideals differ—moral development, practical utility, general culture, discipline, and professional training. These aims are each especially represented in some distinct part of the system of education;

and with the growing interaction of the parts, each is supposed to afford a certain amount of culture, discipline, and utility. But the lack of fundamental unity is witnessed in the fact that one study is still considered good for discipline, and another for culture; some parts of arithmetic, for example, for discipline and others for use, literature for culture, grammar for discipline, geography partly for utility, partly for culture; and so on. The unity of education is dissipated, and the studies become centrifugal; so much of this study to secure this end, so much of that to secure another, until the whole becomes a sheer compromise and patchwork between contending aims and disparate studies. The great problem in education on the administrative side is to secure the unity of the whole, in the place of a sequence of more or less unrelated and overlapping parts and thus to reduce the waste arising from friction, reduplication and transitions that are not properly bridged.

In this second symbolic diagram (II) I wish to suggest that really the only way to unite the parts of the system is to unite each to life. We can get only an artificial unity so long as we confine our gaze to the school system itself. We must look at it as part of the larger whole of social life. This block (A) in the center represents the school system as a whole. (1) At one side we have the

Chart II

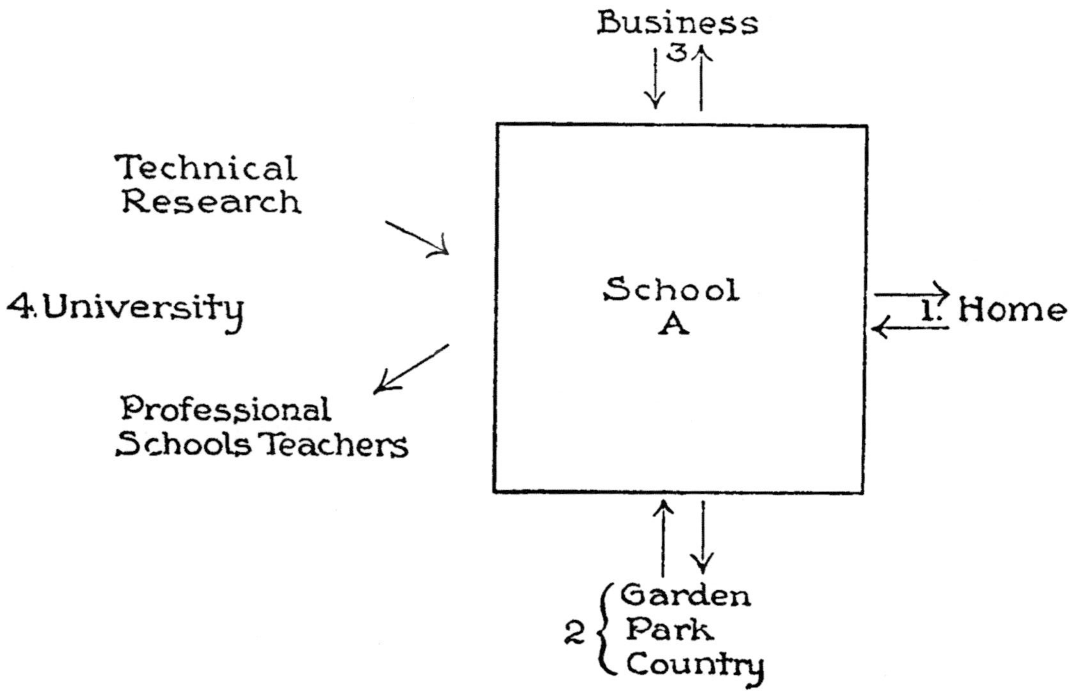

Business
3
Technical
Research
School
A
1. Home
4. University
Professional
Schools Teachers
2
Garden
Park
Country

home, and the two arrows represent the free interplay of influences, materials, and ideas between the home life and that of the school. (2) Below we have the relation to the natural environment, the great field of geography in the widest sense. The school building has about it a natural environment. It ought to be in a garden, and the children from the garden would be led on to surrounding fields, and then into the wider country, with all its facts and forces. (3) Above is represented business life, and the necessity for free play between the school and the needs and forces of industry. (4) On the other side is the university proper, with its various phases, its laboratories, its resources in the way of libraries, museums, and professional schools.

From the standpoint of the child, the great waste in the school comes from his inability to utilize the experiences he gets outside the school in any complete and free way within the school itself; while, on the other hand, he is unable to apply in daily life what he is learning at school. That is the isolation of the school—its isolation from life. When the child gets into the schoolroom he has to put out of his mind a large part of the ideas, interests, and activities that predominate in his home and neighborhood. So the school, being unable to utilize this everyday experience, sets painfully to work, on another tack and by a variety of means, to arouse in the child an interest in school studies. While I was visiting in the city of Moline a few years ago, the superintendent told me that they found many children every year, who were surprised to learn that the Mississippi river in the text-book had anything to do with the stream of water flowing past their homes. The geography being simply a matter of the schoolroom, it is more or less of an awakening to many children to find that the whole thing is nothing but a more formal and definite statement of the facts which they see, feel, and touch every day. When we think that we all live on the earth, that we live in an atmosphere, that our lives are touched at every point by the influences of the soil, flora, and fauna, by considerations of light and heat, and then think of what the school study of geography has been, we have a typical idea of the gap existing between the everyday experiences of the child, and the isolated material supplied in such large measure in the school. This is but an instance, and one upon which most of us may reflect long before we take the present artificiality of the school as other than a matter of course or necessity.

Though there should be organic connection between the school and business life, it is not meant that the school is to prepare the child for any particular business, but that there should be a natural connection of the everyday life of the child with the business environment about him, and that it is the affair of the school to clarify and liberalize this connection, to bring it to consciousness, not by introducing special studies, like commercial geography and arithmetic, but by keeping alive the ordinary bonds of relation. The subject of compound-business-partnership is probably not in many of the arithmetics nowadays, though it was there not a generation ago, for the makers of text-books said that if they left out anything they could not sell their books. This compound-business-partnership originated as far back as the sixteenth century. The joint-stock company had not been invented, and as large commerce with the Indies and Americas grew up, it was necessary to have an accumulation of capital with which to handle it. One man said, "I will put in this amount of money for six months," and another, "So much for two years," and so on. Thus by joining together they got money enough to float their commercial enterprises. Naturally, then, "compound partnership" was taught in the schools. The joint-stock company was invented; compound partnership disappeared, but the problems relating to it stayed in the arithmetics for two hundred years. They were kept after they had ceased to have practical utility, for the sake of mental discipline —

they were "such hard problems, you know." A great deal of what is now in the arithmetics under the head of percentage is of the same nature. Children of twelve and thirteen years of age go through gain and loss calculations, and various forms of bank discount so complicated that the bankers long ago dispensed with them. And when it is pointed out that business is not done this way, we hear again of "mental discipline." And yet there are plenty of real connections between the experience of children and business conditions which need to be utilized and illuminated. The child should study his commercial arithmetic and geography, not as isolated things by themselves, but in their reference to his social environment. The youth needs to become acquainted with the bank as a factor in modern life, with what it does, and how it does it; and then relevant arithmetical processes would have some meaning—quite in contradistinction to the time-absorbing and mind-killing examples in percentage, partial payments, etc., found in all our arithmetics.

The connection with the university, as indicated in this chart, I need not dwell upon. I simply wish to indicate that there ought to be a free interaction between all the parts of the school system. There is much of utter triviality of subject-matter in elementary and secondary education. When we investigate it, we find that it is full of facts taught that are not facts, which have to be unlearned later on. Now, this happens because the "lower" parts of our system are not in vital connection with the "higher." The university or college, in its idea, is a place of research, where investigation is going on, a place of libraries and museums, where the best resources of the past are gathered, maintained and organized. It is, however, as true in the school as in the university that the spirit of inquiry can be got only through and with the attitude of inquiry. The pupil must learn what has meaning, what enlarges his horizon, instead of mere trivialities. He must become acquainted with truths, instead of things that were regarded as such fifty years ago, or that are taken as interesting by the misunderstanding of a partially educated teacher. It is difficult to see how these ends can be reached except as the most advanced part of the educational system is in complete interaction with the most rudimentary.

The next chart (III) is an enlargement of the second. The school building has swelled out, so to speak, the surrounding environment remaining the same, the home, the garden and country, the relation to business life and the university. The object is to show what the school must become to get out of its isolation and secure the organic connection with social life of which we have been speaking. It is not our architect's plan for the school building that we hope to have; but it is a diagrammatic representation of the idea which we want embodied in the school building. On the lower side you see the dining-room and the kitchen, at the top the wood and metal shops, and the textile room for sewing and weaving. The center represents the manner in which all come together in the library; that is to say, in a collection of the intellectual resources of all kinds that throw light upon the practical work, that give it meaning and liberal value. If the four corners represent practice, the interior represents the theory of the practical activities. In other words, the object of these forms of practice in the school is not found chiefly in themselves, or in the technical skill of cooks, seamstresses, carpenters and masons, but in their connection, on the social side, with the life without; while on the individual side they respond to the child's need of action, of expression, of desire to do something, to be constructive and creative, instead of simply passive and conforming. Their great significance is that they keep the balance between the social and individual sides—the chart symbolizing particularly the connection with the social. Here on one side is the home. How naturally the lines of connection play back and forth between the home

Chart III

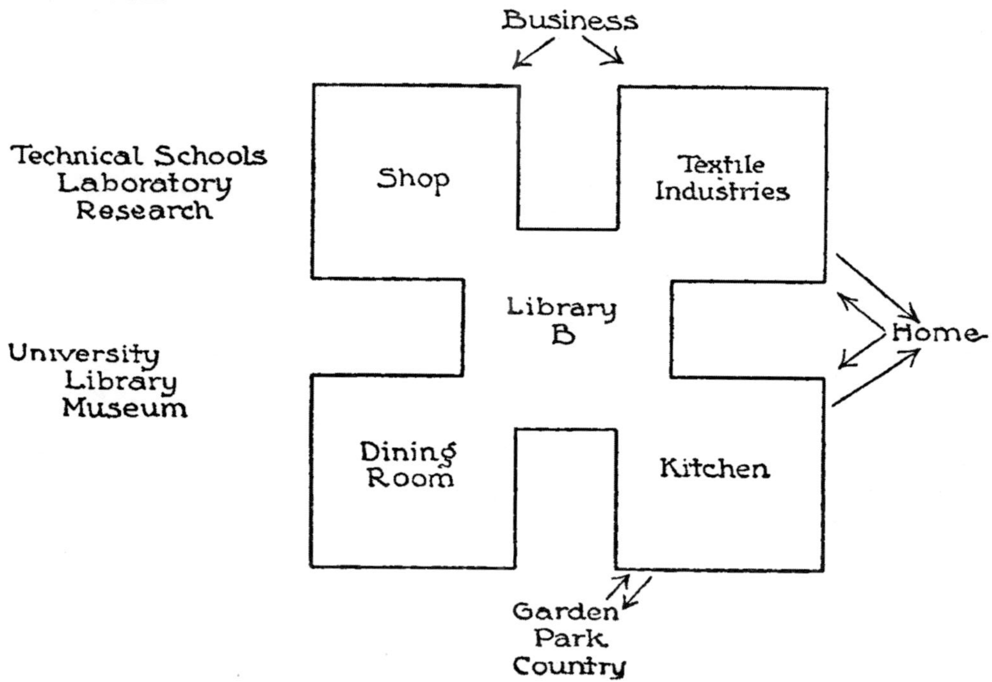
Business
Technical Schools
Laboratory
Research
Shop
Textile
Industries
Library
B
Home
University
Library
Museum
Dining
Room
Kitchen
Garden
Park
Country

and the kitchen and the textile room of the school! The child can carry over what he learns in the home and utilize it in the school; and the things learned in the school he applies at home. These are the two great things in breaking down isolation, in getting connection—to have the child come to school with all the experience he has got outside the school, and to leave it with something to be immediately used in his everyday life. The child comes to the traditional school with a healthy body and a more or less unwilling mind, though, in fact, he does not bring both his body and mind with him; he has to leave his mind behind, because there is no way to use it in the school. If he had a purely abstract mind, he could bring it to school with him, but his is a concrete one, interested in concrete things, and unless these things get over into school life, he cannot take his mind with him. What we want is to have the child come to school with a whole mind and a whole body, and leave school with a fuller mind and an even healthier body. And speaking of the body suggests that, while there is no gymnasium in these diagrams, the active life carried on in its four corners brings with it constant physical exercise, while our gymnasium proper will deal with the particular weaknesses of children and their correction, and will attempt more consciously to build up the thoroughly sound body as the abode of the sound mind.

That the dining-room and kitchen connect with the country and its processes and products it is hardly necessary to say. Cooking may be so taught that it has no connection with country life, and with the sciences that find their unity in geography. Perhaps it generally has been taught without these connections being really made. But all the materials that come into the kitchen have their origin in the country; they come from the soil, are nurtured through the influences of light and water, and represent a great variety of local environments. Through this connection, extending from the garden into the larger world, the child has his most natural introduction to the study of the sciences. Where did these things grow? What was necessary to their growth? What their relation to the soil? What the effect of different climatic conditions? and so on. We all know what the old-fashioned botany was: partly collecting flowers that were pretty, pressing and mounting them; partly pulling these flowers to pieces and giving technical names to the different parts, finding all the different leaves, naming all their different shapes and forms. It was a study of plants without any reference to the soil, to the country, or to growth. In contrast, a real study of plants takes them in their natural environment and in their uses as well, not simply as food, but in all their adaptations to the social life of man. Cooking becomes as well a most natural introduction to the study of chemistry, giving the child here also something which he can at once bring to bear upon his daily experience. I once heard a very intelligent woman say that she could not understand how science could be taught to little children, because she did not see how they could understand atoms and molecules. In other words, since she did not see how highly abstract facts could be presented to the child independently of daily experience, she could not understand how science could be taught at all. Before we smile at this remark, we need to ask ourselves if she is alone in her assumption, or whether it simply formulates almost all of our school practice.

The same relations with the outside world are found in the carpentry and the textile shops. They connect with the country, as the source of their materials, with physics, as the science of applying energy, with commerce and distribution, with art in the development of architecture and decoration. They have also an intimate connection with the university on the side of its technological and engineering schools; with the laboratory, and its scientific methods and results.

To go back to the square which is marked the

library (Chart III, A): if you imagine rooms half in the four corners and half in the library, you will get the idea of the recitation room. That is the place where the children bring the experiences, the problems, the questions, the particular facts which they have found, and discuss them so that new light may be thrown upon them, particularly new light from the experience of others, the accumulated wisdom of the world—symbolized in the library. Here is the organic relation of theory and practice; the child not simply doing things, but getting also the *idea* of what he does; getting from the start some intellectual conception that enters into his practice and enriches it; while every idea finds, directly or indirectly, some application in experience, and has some effect upon life. This, I need hardly say, fixes the position of the "book" or reading in education. Harmful as a substitute for experience, it is all-important in interpreting and expanding experience.

The other chart (IV) illustrates precisely the same idea. It gives the symbolic upper story of this ideal school. In the upper corners are the laboratories; in the lower corners are the studios for art work, both the graphic and auditory arts. The questions, the chemical and physical problems, arising in the kitchen and shop, are taken to the laboratories to be worked out. For instance, this past week one of the older groups

Chart IV

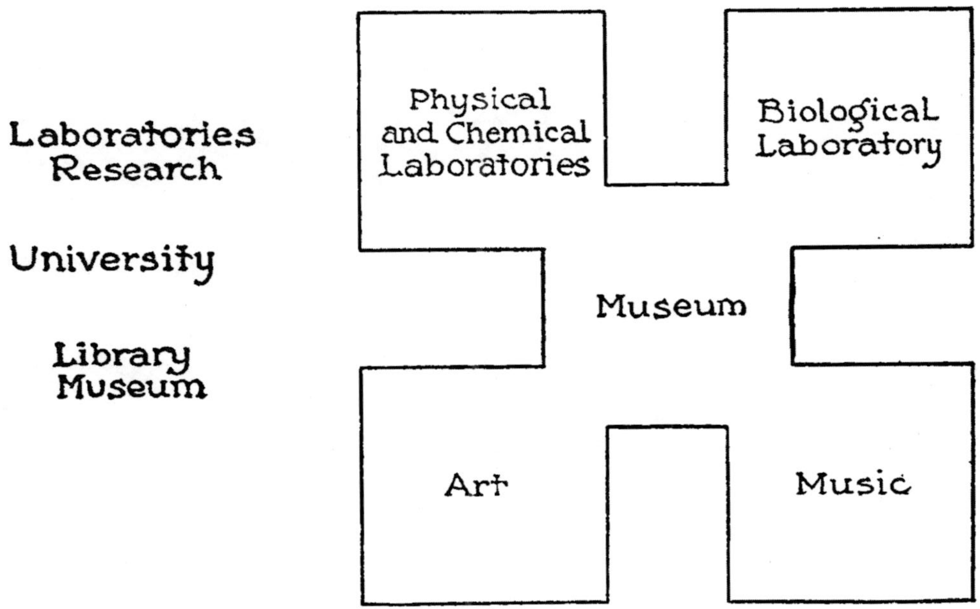
Laboratories
Research
University
Library
Museum
Physical
and Chemical
Laboratories
Biological
Laboratory
Museum
Art
Music

of children doing practical work in weaving which involved the use of the spinning wheel, worked out the diagrams of the direction of forces concerned in treadle and wheel, and the ratio of velocities between wheel and spindle. In the same manner, the plants with which the child has to do in cooking, afford the basis for a concrete interest in botany, and may be taken and studied by themselves. In a certain school in Boston science work for months was centered in the growth of the cotton plant, and yet something new was brought in every day. We hope to do similar work with all the types of plants that furnish materials for sewing and weaving. These examples will suggest, I hope, the relation which the laboratories bear to the rest of the school.

The drawing and music, or the graphic and auditory arts, represent the culmination, the idealization, the highest point of refinement of all the work carried on. I think everybody who has not a purely literary view of the subject recognizes that genuine art grows out of the work of the artisan. The art of the Renaissance was great, because it grew out of the manual arts of life. It did not spring up in a separate atmosphere, however ideal, but carried on to their spiritual meaning processes found in homely and everyday forms of life. The school should observe this relationship. The merely artisan side is narrow, but the mere art, taken by itself, and grafted on from without, tends to become forced, empty, sentimental. I do not mean, of course, that all art work must be correlated in detail to the other work of the school, but simply that a spirit of union gives vitality to the art, and depth and richness to the other work. All art involves physical organs, the eye and hand, the ear and voice; and yet it is something more than the mere technical skill required by the organs of expression. It involves an idea, a thought, a spiritual rendering of things; and yet it is other than any number of ideas by themselves. It is a living union of thought and the instrument of expression. This union is symbolized by saying that in the ideal school the art work might be considered to be that of the shops, passed through the alembic of library and museum into action again.

Take the textile room as an illustration of such a synthesis. I am talking about a future school, the one we hope, some time, to have. The basal fact in that room is that it is a workshop, doing actual things in sewing, spinning, and weaving. The children come into immediate connection with the materials, with various fabrics of silk, cotton, linen and wool. Information at once appears in connection with these materials; their origin, history, their adaptation to particular uses, and the machines of various kinds by which the raw materials are utilized. Discipline arises in dealing with the problems involved, both theoretical and practical. Whence does the culture arise? Partly from seeing all these things reflected through the medium of their scientific and historic conditions and associations, whereby the child learns to appreciate them as technical achievements, as thoughts precipitated in action; and partly because of the introduction of the art idea into the room itself. In the ideal school there would be something of this sort: first, a complete industrial museum, giving samples of materials in various stages of manufacture, and the implements, from the simplest to the most complex, used in dealing with them; then a collection of photographs and pictures illustrating the landscapes and the scenes from which the materials come, their native homes, and their places of manufacture. Such a collection would be a vivid and continual lesson in the synthesis of art, science, and industry. There would be, also, samples of the more perfect forms of textile work, as Italian, French, Japanese, and Oriental. There would be objects illustrating motives of design and decoration which have entered into production. Literature would contribute its part in its idealized representation of the world-industries, as the Penelope in the Odyssey—a classic in literature only because the character is an adequate embodiment of a certain industrial phase of social life. So, from Homer down to the present time, there is a continuous procession of related facts which have been translated into terms of art. Music lends its share, from the Scotch song at the wheel to the spinning song of Marguerite, or of Wagner's Senta. The shop becomes a pictured museum, appealing to the eye. It would have not only materials, beautiful woods and designs, but would give a synopsis of the historical evolution of architecture in its drawings and pictures.

Thus I have attempted to indicate how the school may be connected with life so that the experience gained by the child in a familiar, commonplace way is carried over and made use of there, and what the child learns in the school is carried back and applied in everyday life, making the school an organic whole, instead of a composite of isolated parts. The isolation of studies as well as of parts of the school system disappears. Experience has its geographical aspect, its artistic and its literary, its scientific and its historical sides. All studies arise from aspects of the one earth and the one life lived upon it. We do not have a series of stratified earths, one of which is mathematical, another physical, another historical, and so on. We should not live very long in any one taken by itself. We live in a world where all sides are bound together. All studies grow out of relations in the one great common world. When the child lives in varied but concrete and active relationship to this common world, his studies are naturally unified. It will no longer be a problem to correlate studies. The teacher will not have to resort to all sorts of devices to weave a little arithmetic into the history lesson, and the like. Relate the school to life, and all studies are of necessity correlated.

Moreover, if the school is related as a whole to life as a whole, its various aims and ideals — culture, discipline, information, utility — cease to be variants, for one of which we must select one study and for another another. The growth of the child in the direction of social capacity and service, his larger and more vital union with life, becomes the unifying aim; and discipline, culture and information fall into place as phases of this growth.

I wish to say one word more about the relationship of our particular school to the University. The problem is to unify, to organize education, to bring all its various factors together, through putting it as a whole into organic union with everyday life. That which lies back of the pedagogical school of the University is the necessity of working out something to serve as a model for such unification, extending from work beginning with the four-year-old child up through the graduate work of the University. Already we have much help from the University in scientific work planned, sometimes even in detail, by heads of the departments. The graduate student comes to us with his researches and methods, suggesting ideas and problems. The library and museum are at hand. We want to bring all things educational together; to break down the barriers that divide the education of the little child from the instruction of the maturing youth; to identify the lower and the higher education, so that it shall be demonstrated to the eye that there is no lower and higher, but simply education.

Speaking more especially with reference to the pedagogical side of the work: I suppose the oldest university chair of pedagogy in our country is about twenty years old—that of the University of Michigan, founded in the latter seventies. But there are only one or two that have tried to make a connection between theory and practice. They teach for the most part by theory, by lectures, by reference to books, rather than through the actual work of teaching itself. At Columbia, through the Teachers' College, there is an extensive and close connection between the University and the training of teachers.

Something has been done in one or two other places along the same line. We want an even more intimate union here, so that the University shall put all its resources at the disposition of the elementary school, contributing to the evolution of valuable subject-matter and right method, while the school in turn will be a laboratory in which the student of education sees theories and ideas demonstrated, tested, criticised, enforced, and the evolution of new truths. We want the school in its relation to the University to be a working model of a unified education.

A word as to the relation of the school to educational interests generally. I heard once that the adoption of a certain method in use in our school was objected to by a teacher on this ground: "You know that it is an experimental school. They do not work under the same conditions that we are subject to." Now, the purpose of performing an experiment is that other people need not experiment; at least need not experiment so much, may have something definite and positive to go by. An experiment demands particularly favorable conditions in order that results may be reached both freely and securely. It has to work unhampered, with all the needed resources at command. Laboratories lie back of all the great business enterprises of today, back of every great factory, every railway and steamship system. Yet the laboratory is not a business enterprise; it does not aim to secure for itself the conditions of business life, nor does the commercial undertaking repeat the laboratory. There is a difference between working out and testing a new truth, or a new method, and applying it on a wide scale, making it available for the mass of men, making it commercial. But the first thing is to discover the truth, to afford all necessary facilities, for this is the most practical thing in the world in the long run. We do not expect to have other schools literally imitate what we do. A working model is not something to be copied; it is to afford a demonstration of the feasibility of the principle, and of the methods which make it feasible. So (to come back to our own point) we want here to work out the problem of the unity, the organization of the school system in itself, and to do this by relating it so intimately to life as to demonstrate the possibility and necessity of such organization for all education.

THREE YEARS OF THE UNIVERSITY ELEMENTARY SCHOOL

IV

THREE YEARS OF THE UNIVERSITY ELEMENTARY SCHOOL[1]

The school was started the first week in January, three years ago. I shall try this afternoon to give a brief statement of the ideas and problems that were in mind when the experiment was started, and a sketch of the development of the work since that time. We began in a small house in Fifty-seventh street, with fifteen children. We found ourselves the next year with twenty-five children in Kimbark avenue, and then moved in January to Rosalie court, the larger quarters enabling us to take forty children. The next year the numbers increased to sixty, the school remaining at Rosalie court. This year we have had ninety-five on the roll at one time, and are located at 5412 Ellis avenue, where we hope to stay till we have a building and grounds of our own.

The children during the first year of the school were between the ages of six and nine. Now

[1] Stenographic report of a talk by John Dewey at a meeting of the Parents' Association of the University Elementary School, February, 1899; somewhat revised.

their ages range between four and thirteen—the members of the oldest group being in their thirteenth year. This is the first year that we have children under six, and this has been made possible through the liberality of friends in Honolulu, H. I., who are building up there a memorial kindergarten along the same lines.

The expenses of the school during the first year, of two terms only, were between $1,300 and $1,400. The expenses this year will be about $12,000. Of this amount $5,500 will come from tuitions; $5,000 has been given by friends interested in the school, and there remains about $1,500 yet to be raised for the conduct of the school. This is an indication of the increase of expenses. The average expense per pupil is about the same since the start, *i. e.*, $120 per child per school year. Relatively speaking, this year the expenses of the school took something of a jump, through the expense of moving to a new building, and the repairs and changes there necessary. An increase in the staff of teachers has also enlarged the work as well as the debits of the school. Next year (1899–1900) we hope to have about 120 children, and apparently the expenses will be about $2,500 more than this. Of this amount $2,000 will be met by the increase in tuition from the pupils. The cost of a child to the school, $120 a year, is precisely the tuition charged by the University for students and is double the average tuition charged by the school. But it is not expected that the University tuition will come anywhere near meeting the expense involved there. One reason for not increasing the tuition here, even if it were advisable for other reasons, is that it is well to emphasize, from an educational point of view, that elementary as well as advanced education requires endowment. There is every reason why money should be spent freely for the organization and maintenance of foundation work in education as well as for the later stages.

The elementary school has had from the outset two sides: one, the obvious one of instruction of the children who have been intrusted to it; the other, relationship to the University, since the school is under the charge, and forms a part of the pedagogical work of the University.

When the school was started, there were certain ideas in mind — perhaps it would be better to say questions and problems; certain points which it seemed worth while to test. If you will permit one personal word, I should like to say that it is sometimes thought that the school started out with a number of ready-made principles and ideas which were to be put into practice at once. It has been popularly assumed that I am the author of these ready-made ideas and principles which were to go into execution. I take this opportunity to say that the educational conduct of the school, as well as its administration, the selection of subject-matter, and the working out of the course of study, as well as actual instruction of children, have been almost entirely in the hands of the teachers of the school; and that there has been a gradual development of the educational principles and methods involved, not a fixed equipment. The teachers started with question marks, rather than with fixed rules, and if any answers have been reached, it is the teachers in the school who have supplied them. We started upon the whole with four such questions, or problems:

1. What can be done, and how can it be done, to bring the school into closer relation with the home and neighborhood life—instead of having the school a place where the child comes solely to learn certain lessons? What can be done to break down the barriers which have unfortunately come to separate the school life from the rest of the everyday life of the child? This does not mean, as it is sometimes, perhaps, interpreted to mean, that the child should simply take up in the school things already experienced at home and study them, but that, so far as possible, the child shall have the same attitude and point of view in the school as in the home; that he shall

find the same interest in going to school, and in there doing things worth doing for their own sake, that he finds in the plays and occupations which busy him in his home and neighborhood life. It means, again, that the motives which keep the child at work and growing at home shall be used in the school, so that he shall not have to acquire another set of principles of actions belonging only to the school—separate from those of the home. It is a question of the unity of the child's experience, of its actuating motives and aims, not of amusing or even interesting the child.

2. What can be done in the way of introducing subject-matter in history and science and art, that shall have a positive value and real significance in the child's own life; that shall represent, even to the youngest children, something worthy of attainment in skill or knowledge; as much so to the little pupil as are the studies of the high-school or college student to him? You know what the traditional curriculum of the first few years is, even though many modifications have been made. Some statistics have been collected showing that 75 or 80 per cent. of the first three years of a child in school are spent upon the form — not the substance — of learning, the mastering of the symbols of reading, writing, and arithmetic. There is not much positive nutriment in this. Its purpose is important — is

necessary—but it does not represent the same kind of increase in a child's intellectual and moral experience that is represented by positive truth of history and nature, or by added insight into reality and beauty. One thing, then, we wanted to find out is how much can be given a child that is really worth his while to get, in knowledge of the world about him, of the forces in the world, of historical and social growth, and in capacity to express himself in a variety of artistic forms. From the strictly educational side this has been the chief problem of the school. It is along this line that we hope to make our chief contribution to education in general; we hope, that is, to work out and publish a positive body of subject-matter which may be generally available.

3. How can instruction in these formal, symbolic branches—the mastering of the ability to read, write, and use figures intelligently—be carried on with everyday experience and occupation as their background and in definite relations to other studies of more inherent content, and be carried on in such a way that the child shall feel their necessity through their connection with subjects which appeal to him on their own account? If this can be accomplished, he will have a vital motive for getting the technical capacity. It is not meant, as has been sometimes jocosely stated, that the child learn to bake and

sew at school, and to read, write, and figure at home. It is intended that these formal subjects shall not be presented in such large doses at first as to be the exclusive objects of attention, and that the child shall be led by that which he is doing to feel the need for acquiring skill in the use of symbols and the immediate power they give. In any school, if the child realizes the motive for the use and application of number and language he has taken the longest step toward securing the power; and he can realize the motive only as he has some particular — not some general and remote — use for the symbols.

4. Individual attention. This is secured by small groupings — eight or ten in a class — and a large number of teachers supervising systematically the intellectual needs and attainments and physical well-being and growth of the child. To secure this we have now 135 hours of instructors' time per week, that is, the time of nine teachers for three hours per day, or one teacher per group. It requires but a few words to make this statement about attention to individual powers and needs, and yet the whole of the school's aims and methods, moral, physical, intellectual, are bound up in it.

I think these four points present a fair statement of what we have set out to discover. The school is often called an experimental school, and in one sense that is the proper name. I do not like to use it too much, for fear parents will think we are experimenting upon the children, and that they naturally object to. But it is an experimental school—at least I hope so—with reference to education and educational problems. We have attempted to find out by trying, by doing—not alone by discussion and theorizing—*whether* these problems may be worked out, and *how* they may be worked out.

Next a few words about the means that have been used in the school in order to test these four questions, and to supply their answers, and first as to the place given to hand-work of different kinds in the school. There are three main lines regularly pursued: (*a*) the shop-work with wood and tools, (*b*) cooking work, and (*c*) work with textiles—sewing and weaving. Of course, there is other hand-work in connection with science, as science is largely of an experimental nature. It is a fact that may not have come to your attention that a large part of the best and most advanced scientific work involves a great deal of manual skill, the training of the hand and eye. It is impossible for one to be a first-class worker in science without this training in manipulation, and in handling apparatus and materials. In connection with the history work, especially with the younger children, hand-work is brought in in the way of making implements, weapons, tools, etc. Of course, the art work is another side—drawing, painting, and modeling. Logically, perhaps, the gymnasium work does not come in here, but as a means of developing moral and intellectual control through the medium of the body it certainly does. The children have one-half hour per day of this form of physical exercise. Along this line we have found that hand-work, in large variety and amount, is the most easy and natural method of keeping up the same attitude of the child in and out of the school. The child gets the largest part of his acquisitions through his bodily activities, until he learns to work systematically with the intellect. That is the purpose of this work in the school, to direct these activities, to systematize and organize them, so that they shall not be as haphazard and as wandering as they are outside of school. The problem of making these forms of practical activity work continuously and definitely together, leading from one factor of skill to another, from one intellectual difficulty to another, has been one of the most difficult, and at the same time one in which we have been most successful. The various kinds of work, carpentry, cooking, sewing, and weaving, are selected as involving different kinds of skill, and demanding different types of intellectual attitude on the part of the child, and because they represent some of the most important activities of the everyday outside world: the question of living under shelter, of daily food and clothing, of the home, of personal movement and exchange of goods. He gets also the training of sense organs, of touch, of sight, and the ability to coördinate eye and hand. He gets healthy exercise; for the child demands a much larger amount of physical activity than the formal program of the ordinary school permits. There is also a continual appeal to memory, to judgment, in adapting ends to means, a training in habits of order, industry, and neatness in the care of the tools and utensils, and in doing things in a systematic, instead of a haphazard, way. Then, again, these practical occupations make a background, especially in the earlier groups, for the later studies. The children get a good deal of chemistry in connection with cooking, of number work and geometrical principles in carpentry, and a good deal of geography in connection with their theoretical work in weaving and sewing. History also comes in with the origin and growth of various inventions, and their effects upon social life and political organization.

Perhaps more attention, upon the whole, has been given to our second point, that of positive subject-matter, than to any one other thing. On the history side the curriculum is now fairly well worked out. The younger children begin with the home and occupations of the home. In the sixth year the intention is that the children should study occupations outside the home, the larger social industries — farming, mining, lumber, etc.— that they may see the complex and various social industries on which life depends, while incidentally they investigate the use of the various materials—woods, metals, and the processes applied— thus getting a beginning of scientific study. The next year is given to the historical development of industry and invention — starting with man as a savage and carrying him through the typical phases of his progress upward, until the iron age is reached and man begins to enter upon a civilized career. The object of the study of primitive life is not to keep the child interested in lower and relatively savage stages, but to show him the steps of progress and development, especially along the line of invention, by which man was led into civilization. There is a certain nearness, after all, in the child to primitive forms of life. They are much more simple than existing institutions. By throwing the emphasis upon the progress of man, and upon the way advance has been made, we hope to avoid the objections that hold against paying too much attention to the crudities and distracting excitements of savage life.

The next two or three years, *i. e.*, the fourth and fifth grades, and perhaps the sixth, will be devoted to American history. It is then that history, properly speaking, begins, as the study of primitive life can hardly be so called.

Then comes Greek history and Roman, in the regular chronological order, each year having its own work planned with reference to what has come before and after.

The science work was more difficult to arrange and systematize, because there was so little to follow—so little that has been already done in an organized way. We are now at work upon a program,[1] and I shall not speak in detail about it. The first two or three years cultivate the children's powers of observation, lead them to sympathetic interest in the habits of plants and animals, and to look at things with reference to their uses. Then the center of the work becomes geographical—the study of the earth, as the most central thing. From this almost all the work grows out, and to it the work goes back. Another standpoint in the science work is that of the application of natural forces to the service of man through machines. Last year a good deal of work

[1] This year's program is published in the *Elementary School Record.* Address The University of Chicago Press for particulars.

was done in electricity (and will be repeated this year), based on the telegraph and telephone—taking up the things that can easily be grasped.

In mechanics they have studied locks and clocks with reference to the adaptation of the various parts of the machinery. All this work makes a most excellent basis for more formal physics later on. Cooking gives opportunity for getting a great many ideas of heat and water, and of their effects. The scientific work taken up in the school differs mainly from that of other schools in having the experimental part—physics and chemistry—emphasized, and is not confined simply to nature study—the study of plants and animals. Not that the latter is less valuable, but that we find it possible to introduce the physical aspects from the first.

If I do not spend a large amount of time in speaking of the music and art work, it is not because they are not considered valuable and important—certainly as much so as any other work done in the school, not only in the development of the child's moral and æsthetic nature, but also from a strictly intellectual point of view. I know of no work in the school that better develops the power of attention, the habit of observation and of consecutiveness, of seeing parts in relation to a whole.

I shall now say a few words about the administrative side of the school. At the outset we mixed up the children of different ages and attainments as much as possible, believing there were mental advantages in the give-and-take thus secured, as well as the moral advantages in having the older assume certain responsibilities in the care of the younger. As the school grew, it became necessary to abandon the method, and to group the children with reference to their common capacities. These groupings, however, are based, not on ability to read and write, but upon similarity of mental attitude and interest, and upon general intellectual capacity and mental alertness. There are ways in which we are still trying to carry out the idea of mixing up the children, that we may not build the rigid step-ladder system of the "graded" school. One step in this direction is having the children move about and come in contact with different teachers. While there are difficulties and evils connected with this, I think one of the most useful things in the school is that children come into intimate relation with a number of different personalities. The children also meet in general assemblies—for singing, and for the report of the whole school work as read by members of the different groups. The older children are also given a half hour a week in which to join some of the younger groups, and, if possible, as in handwork, enter into the work of the younger children. In various ways we are attempting to keep a family spirit throughout the school, and not the feeling of isolated classes and grades.

The organization of the teaching force has gradually become departmental, as the needs of the work have indicated its chief branches. So we now have recognized divisions of Science, History, Domestic or Household Arts, Manual Training in the limited sense (wood and metals), Music, Art (that is, drawing, water colors, clay modeling, etc.), and Gymnasium. As the work goes on into the secondary period, the languages and mathematics will also of necessity assume a more differentiated and distinct position. As it is sometimes said that correlated or thoroughly harmonized work cannot be secured upon this basis, I am happy to say that our experience shows positively that there are no intrinsic difficulties. Through common devotion to the best development of the child, through common loyalty to the main aims and methods of the school, our teachers have demonstrated that in education, as in business, the best organization is secured through proper regard for natural divisions of labor, interest, and training. The child secures the advantage in discipline and knowledge of contact with experts in each line, while the individual teachers serve the common thought in diverse ways, thus multiplying and re-inforcing it.

Upon the moral side, that of so-called discipline and order, where the work of the University Elementary School has perhaps suffered most from misunderstanding and misrepresentation, I shall say only that our ideal has been, and continues to be, that of the best form of family life, rather than that of a rigid graded school. In the latter, the large number of children under the care of a single teacher, and the very limited number of modes of activity open to the pupils, have made necessary certain fixed and somewhat external forms of "keeping order." It would be very stupid to copy these, under the changed conditions of our school, its small groups permitting and requiring the most intimate personal acquaintance of child and teacher, and its great variety of forms of work, with their differing adaptations to the needs of different children. If we have permitted to our children more than the usual amount of freedom, it has not been in order to relax or decrease real discipline, but because under our particular conditions larger and less artificial responsibilities could thus be required of the children, and their entire development of body and spirit be more harmonious and complete. And I am confident that the parents who have intrusted their children to us for any length of time will agree in saying that, while the children like, or love, to come to school, yet work, and not amusement, has been the spirit and teaching of the school; and that this freedom has been granted under such conditions of intelligent and sympathetic oversight as to be a means of upbuilding and strengthening character.

At the end of three years, then, we are not afraid to say that some of our original questions have secured affirmative answers. The increase of our children from fifteen to almost one hundred, along with a practical doubling of fees, has shown that parents are ready for a form of education that makes individual growth its sole controlling aim. The presence of an organized corps of instructors demonstrates that thoroughly educated teachers are ready to bring to elementary education the same resources of training, knowledge, and skill that have long been at the command of higher education. The everyday work of the school shows that children can live in school as out of it, and yet grow daily in wisdom, kindness, and the spirit of obedience — that learning may, even with little children, lay hold upon the substance of truth that nourishes the spirit, and yet the forms of knowledge be observed and cultivated; and that growth may be genuine and thorough, and yet a delight.